THE ILL-EFFE

Sins

by
Shaykh Muhammad ibn Saalih al-'Uthaymeen

Translated by
Aboo Talhah Daawood ibn Ronald Burbank

ISBN 1 898649 04 9

British Library Cataloguing in Publication Data.

A catalogue record for this book is available from the British Library.

© Copyright 1994 by Al-Hidaayah Publishing & Distribution

Printed by Interprint Limited

Typeset by Al-Hidaayah Publishing & Distribution

Cover design by Karra Design & Print

Published by: Al-Hidaayah Publishing & Distribution
                  P.O. Box 3332
                  Birmingham
                  United Kingdom
                  B10 0UH

                  Tel: 0121 753 1889
                  Fax: 0121 753 2422
                  Email: mail@al-hidaayah.co.uk
                  Website: www.al-hidaayah.co.uk

Publisher's Note

All praise is for Allaah, Lord of the worlds. Peace and blessings be upon Muhammad, his family, his Companions and all those who follow in their footsteps until the Last Day. To proceed...

In an age of materialism when everything that happens is attributed to materialistic causes, we hope that this booklet will help to correct the misunderstandings of many of our brothers and sisters who fail to realise the consequences of sins and disobedience to Allaah, the Most High. We pray that this realisation results in the Muslims as a whole becoming better slaves of Allaah, the Mighty and Majestic, by abstaining from sins and disobedience and turning to the worship of Him alone - *aameen*.

This short booklet is a translation of a *khutbah* (sermon) delivered by Shaykh Muhammad ibn Saalih al-'Uthaymeen on the 12th of Muharram in the year 1411AH. which has been published in Arabic under the title: *Athar ul-Ma'aasee 'Alal Fardi Wal Mujtama.'*

Shaykh Muhammad ibn Saalih al-'Uthaymeen is one of the leading scholars of *Ahlus-Sunnah-wal-Jamaa'ah* of our time. He has authored many books on various subjects including *'Aqeedah* and *Fiqh*.

May Allaah make this treatise of benefit to those who read it, and may He reward all those who helped in its production - *aameen*.

Al-Hidaayah Publishing & Distribution

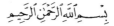

All praise is for Allaah, in whose Hand is the dominion of the heavens and the earth. Sovereignty is His, all praise is for Him, and He is a witness of everything. All His prescribed laws and what He has decreed are from His Wisdom. He does whatever He wills and commands whatever He wishes. I testify that none has the right to be worshipped except Allaah alone, having no partner, the Guardian, the One Worthy of all Praise. I testify that Muhammad is His slave and Messenger, the last of the prophets and their leader and the best of worshippers; may Allaah extol and send complete peace upon his family, his Companions and those who follow them in goodness till the Day of Judgement. To proceed...

Allaah, the Mighty and Majestic, says, explaining His complete Power, and perfect Wisdom, that what He alone orders is what happens, and that He is the one governing and controlling His servants - granting security, fear, ease, hardship, facility, difficulty, straightened circumstances or prosperity... Allaah, the Mighty and Majestic, says:

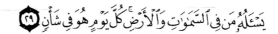

"Whosoever is in the heavens and on earth begs of Him. Every day He has a matter to bring forth (such as giving honour to some, disgrace to some, life to some, death to some etc)!"[1]

So Allaah, the Most High, controls the affairs of His creation enforcing His rulings sometimes according to His Wisdom and Beneficence, and sometimes according to His Wisdom and Justice, and your Lord never treats anyone unjustly:

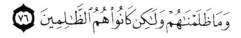

---

[1] Soorah ar-Rahmaan (55):29

"We wronged them not, but they were the wrong-doers."[2]

O Muslims:

Indeed we believe in Allaah and His predecree[3] (*Qadr*), and belief in Allaah's predecree is one of the pillars of *eemaan*.[4] We believe that whatever good or state of ease and security comes upon us, then it is from Allaah's blessings upon us and it is an obligation upon us that we give praise and thanks to the One who granted and provided that for us. This is done by returning to obedience to Him, avoiding whatever He forbade and doing whatever He ordered. If we carry out our duty of obedience to Allaah then we will be giving thanks for His blessings and would then deserve the increase in these blessings which Allaah has promised us from His bounty. Allaah, the Mighty and Majestic, says:

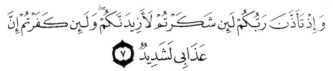

"And whatever of the blessings and good things you have, it is from Allaah."[5]

and He, the Most High, says:

وَإِذْ تَأَذَّنَ رَبُّكُمْ لَئِن شَكَرْتُمْ لَأَزِيدَنَّكُمْ وَلَئِن كَفَرْتُمْ إِنَّ عَذَابِى لَشَدِيدٌ ۝

"And (remember) when your Lord proclaimed: 'If you give thanks, I will give you more (of My blessings), but if you are thankless, verily My punishment is indeed severe.'"[6]

---

2 Soorah az-Zukhruf (43):76

3 For further information on this important branch of belief refer to *Faith in Predestination* by Dr. Suhaib Hasan based on an article by Shaikh Muhammad ibn Saalih al-'Uthaymeen (Al-Qur'an Society, London, 1991). [Publisher's note]

4 *Eemaan* is belief in the heart, saying of the tongue and action of the limbs. [Translator's note]

5 Soorah an-Nahl (16):53

6 Soorah Ibraaheem (14):7

O Muslims:

Alhamdulillaah,[7] we live in this land in a state of security and ease, but this state of security and ease cannot continue except through obedience to Allaah. As long as we order good and forbid evil, as long as we cooperate in ordering good and forbidding evil, since those who order good and forbid evil are at the forefront of the Ummah,[8] and they repel the causes of punishment and chastisement, so we should assist them and be with them. If they err we should inform them of their mistake and warn them about it and lead them to the guidance and not let their mistake become a reason to remove and distance them from this responsibility - that is not the correct way...

O Muslims:

Whatever harm and hardship has befallen the people in their wealth or security, individuals or societies is due to their sins and their having neglected the commands of Allaah and his prescribed laws, and their seeking judgement amongst the people by other than the prescribed laws of Allaah - who created all of creation and was more merciful to them than their mothers and fathers, and He is the One who knows better than themselves what is most beneficial for them.

O Muslims:

I repeat this sentence because of its importance and because many of the people turn away from it:

I say: whatever harm and hardship has befallen the people in their wealth or security, individuals or societies is due to their sins and their having neglected the commands of Allaah and his prescribed laws, and their seeking judgement amongst the people by other than the prescribed laws of Allaah - who created all of creation and was more merciful to them than their mothers and fathers, and He is the One who knows better than themselves what is most beneficial for them.

---

7 All praise and thanks are for Allaah.

8 Ummah: 'Nation', the Muslims as a group.

Allaah, the Mighty and Majestic, says, explaining that in His Book, so that we may realise and take warning, He, the Majestic and Most High, says:

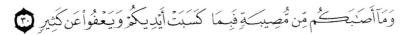

"And whatever of misfortune befalls you, it is because of what your hands have earned. And He pardons much."[9]

and He, the Most High, says:

مَّآ أَصَابَكَ مِنْ حَسَنَةٍ فَمِنَ ٱللَّهِ وَمَآ أَصَابَكَ مِن سَيِّئَةٍ فَمِن نَّفْسِكَ

"Whatever of good reaches you, is from Allaah, but whatever of evil befalls you, is from yourself."[10]

Whatever good comes upon us - blessings or security - it is from Allaah, it is He who provided that, its beginning and end, from His beneficience. It is He who granted us from His bounty that we should carry out that which would lead to it, and it is He who granted us His blessings and completed that for us...

As for whatever evil has befallen us, whether famine or fear, or whatever else causes harm, then it is due to our ownselves, we are the ones who have wronged ourselves and led ourselves to destruction.

O people:
Many people today attribute the misfortunes which befall them, whether relating to wealth and economics, or security and political affairs to purely materialistic causes, to political causes, economic reasons, or problems due to borders. There is no doubt that this is due to their limited understanding and weakness of their *eemaan* and their faliure to reflect upon the Book of

---

9 Soorah ash-Shoora (42):30

10 Soorah an-Nisaa' (4):79

Allaah and the *Sunnah*[11] of His Messenger (ﷺ).

O Muslims, Believers in Allaah and His Messenger (ﷺ):
Behind these reasons are causes prescribed as such by Allaah, reasons and causes for these misfortunes which are stronger, greater and produce a more severe effect than the material reasons. However the material reasons may be a means of bringing about what is due to the causes prescribed by Allaah which necessitates the misfortune and punishment. Allaah, the Mighty and Majestic says:

$$ظَهَرَ ٱلْفَسَادُ فِى ٱلْبَرِّ وَٱلْبَحْرِ بِمَا كَسَبَتْ أَيْدِى ٱلنَّاسِ لِيُذِيقَهُم بَعْضَ ٱلَّذِى عَمِلُواْ لَعَلَّهُمْ يَرْجِعُونَ ﴿٤١﴾$$

"Evil (sins and disobedience of Allaah etc.) has appeared on the land and sea because of what the hands of men have earned (by oppression and evil deeds etc.), that Allaah may make them taste a part of that which they have done, in order that they may return (by repenting to Allaah)."[12]

O people, O Muslims, O nation of Muhammad (ﷺ):
Give thanks for the blessings of Allaah upon you which you are about to hear of. O nation of Muhammad (ﷺ) you are the best and most noble of the nations of Allaah, the Mighty and Majestic. Allaah does not punish this nation for its disobedience and sins in the way that He punished the previous nations. He will not cause its destruction with a single overwhelming punishment as happened to 'Aad,[13] when they were destroyed by the violent wind which He unleashed upon them for seven nights and eight days in succession so that they were left lying like the hollow trunks of palm trees - do you see any remnants of them? He will not destroy it with the like of the punishment of

---

[11] *Sunnah*: The way of life of the Prophet (ﷺ) consisting of his words, actions and silent approvals. The *Sunnah* is contained in the various authentic *ahaadeeth*.

[12] Soorah ar-Room (30):41

[13] See Soorah al-Haaqqah (69): 6-7

Thamood[14] who were seized by the terrible shout and the earthquake so that they lay prostrate corpses in their homes. And He will not destroy it with the like of the punishment of the people of Loot,[15] against whom Allaah sent a violent wind and stones from the sky and turned their homes upside down.

O Muslims:
Allaah, from His Wisdom and His Mercy, punishes this nation for its sins and disobedience by setting some part of it upon the others so that they destroy one another and take each other prisoner. Allaah, the Mighty and Majestic, says:

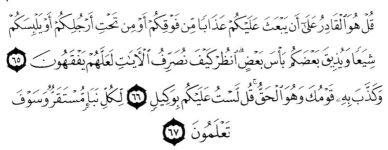

"Say: 'He has power to send torment on you from above you or from under your feet, or to cover you with confusion in party strife, and make you to taste the violence of one another.' See how variously We explain the Ayaat,[16] so that they may understand. But your people (O Muhammad (ﷺ)) have denied it (the Qur'aan) though it is the Truth. Say: 'I am not responsible for your affairs.' For every news there is a fact (i.e. for everything there is an appointed term and you will come to know)."[17]

---

14 See Soorah al-Haaqqah (69): 5

15 See Soorah al-A'raaf (7):80-84

16 Aayaat (sing. aayah): proofs; signs; evidences; lessons; 'verses'.

17 Soorah al-An'aam (6):65-66

Al-Haafidh Ibn Katheer quotes a number of *ahaadeeth*[18] in his *Tafseer* of the first *aayah*. From these is that reported by al-Bukhaaree from Jaabir ibn 'Abdullaah (*radiyallaahu 'anhumaa*) who said:

"When the (following) *aayah* was revealed:

$$قُلْ هُوَ ٱلْقَادِرُ عَلَىٰٓ أَن يَبْعَثَ عَلَيْكُمْ عَذَابًا مِّن فَوْقِكُمْ$$

"Say: 'He has power to send torment on you from above you...'"

The Prophet (ﷺ) said: 'I seek refuge with Your Face.'

$$أَوْ مِن تَحْتِ أَرْجُلِكُمْ$$

"...or from under your feet..."

The Prophet (ﷺ) said: 'I seek refuge with Your Face.'

$$أَوْ يَلْبِسَكُمْ شِيَعًا وَيُذِيقَ بَعْضَكُم بَأْسَ بَعْضٍ$$

"or to cover you with confusion in party strife, and make you to taste the violence of one another."

The Prophet (ﷺ) said: 'This is lighter' or '...easier.'"[19]

It is reported by Muslim from Sa'd ibn Abee Waqqaas, (*radiyallaahu 'anhu*) who said: "We went along with Allaah's Messenger (ﷺ) until we came to the mosque of Banoo Mu'aawiyah, so Allaah's Messenger (ﷺ) entered and prayed two *rak'ahs* so we prayed along with him. So he called upon his Lord for a long time, then he said: 'I asked my Lord for three things: I asked Him

---

[18] *Ahaadeeth* (sing. *hadeeth*): Sayings narrated from the Prophet (ﷺ), regarding his words actions or attributes.

[19] Reported by al-Bukhaaree in his *Saheeh* [Eng. trans. vol. 6, p.120-121 no. 152].

that He should not destroy my nation with a deluge so He granted me that; I asked him that He should not destroy my nation with famine - as happened to the people of Fir'awn so He granted me that; and I asked Him that they should not fight amongst themselves - but He refused me that.'"

From Khabbaab ibn al-Aratt, (radiyallaahu 'anhu), who said: "I came to Allaah's Messenger (ﷺ) on a night in which he spent the whole of it in prayer until it was fajr, so Allaah's Messenger (ﷺ) concluded his prayer with tasleem. I said: 'O Messenger of Allaah: You have prayed a prayer this night the like of which I have not seen you pray.' Allaah's Messenger (ﷺ) said: 'Indeed it was a prayer of hope and fear. In it I asked my Lord, the Mighty and Majestic, for three things, He granted me two and refused me one. I asked my Lord, the Mighty and Majestic, that He should not destroy us with that which He destroyed the nations before us - and He granted it to me; I asked my Lord, the Mighty and Majestic, that He should not overwhelm us with an enemy from other than us - so He granted it to me; and I asked my Lord, the Mighty and Majestic, that He should not cause us to divide into separate groups, each attacking the others, but He refused me that.'" Reported by Imaam Ahmad, an-Nasaa'ee and at-Tirmidhee.

You believe in these Aayaat and you believe in the narrations which are authentic from Allaah's Messenger (ﷺ) so why will you not reflect upon them? Why will you not reflect upon them?

Why will you not attribute these misfortunes which occur to deficiency in your own practice of the Deen so that you turn back to your Lord and save yourselves from the causes of overwhelming destruction?

So fear Allaah O servant of Allaah and look to your affairs and repent before your Lord and correct your way towards Him. Know O nation that these punishments which have come upon you and these trials that have been inflicted upon you are your own doing and due to your sins. So for each chastisement repent and turn to Allaah and seek the refuge of Allaah, the Most High, from the trials; the material trials relating to the person: killing, injury and being forced from ones home; trials relating to wealth: decrease and loss; and trials relating to the *Deen*[20] - the doubts and desires which assail the hearts and keep the *Ummah* away from the *Deen* of Allaah, and keep it away from the way of our Pious Predecessors (*Salaf*) and which lead it to destruction. The trials of the heart are the worst and the most severe of all the trials in this world since worldly misfortunes when they occur can only cause loss in this world, which will pass away anyway, whether sooner or later but trials relating to the *Deen* cause loss of this world and the Hereafter:

قُلْ إِنَّ ٱلْخَٰسِرِينَ ٱلَّذِينَ خَسِرُوٓاْ أَنفُسَهُمْ وَأَهْلِيهِمْ يَوْمَ ٱلْقِيَٰمَةِ أَلَا ذَٰلِكَ هُوَ ٱلْخُسْرَانُ ٱلْمُبِينُ

"Say (O Muhammad (ﷺ)) : The losers are those who will lose themselves and their families on the Day of Ressurection. Verily, that will be a manifest loss!"[21]

O Allaah, we ask you whilst awaiting fulfilment of one of the duties You have made obligatory upon us - that You make us of those who take heed of Your Signs and receive admonition when Your punishment descends.

O Allaah, grant that the Islamic *Ummah* and its leaders truly turn back to You in open and in secret, in their sayings and their actions so that the *Ummah* is rectified, since rectitude of the rulers is a cause of the rectitude of the *Ummah*.

O Allaah, we ask that You rectify those in charge of the affairs of the Muslims and that You grant that they are able to take heed from events and that You direct them to that which You love and is pleasing to You - O Lord of the worlds.

O Allaah, we ask You that you keep away from them every evil adviser - indeed You have full power over everything.

---

[20] The way of life prescribed by Allaah.

[21] Soorah az-Zumur (39):15

O Allaah, guide them through good advisers to that which is good - those who will advise them and encouarage them in good - O Lord of all the worlds.

O Allaah, whoever amongst the advisers of those in authority over the Muslims is not a sincere adviser to them, and is not sincere to the people then remove them and replace them with those who are better than them - O Lord of all the worlds, O Possessor of Majesty and Nobility.

All praise is for Allaah, Lord of all the worlds, and may He extol and send peace upon our Prophet Muhammad, upon his family, true followers and all his Companions. *Aameen.*

The Second Khutbah

All praise is for Allaah, many pure and blessed praises as our Lord loves and is pleased with, and I testify that none has the right to be worshipped except Allaah, alone, having no partner. All praise is for Him at the beginning and the end. I testify that Muhammad is His slave and His Messenger, the one whom He chose and took as His *khaleel*, may Allaah extol him and send peace upon him, his family, followers, Companions and those who follow in his way. To proceed:

O servant of Allaah! Fear Allaah, the Mighty and Majestic, and beware of neglecting the prescribed laws of Allaah... beware of neglecting Allaah's signs... beware of failing to reflect upon the Book of Allaah... beware of failing to know the *Sunnah* of Allaah's Messenger (ﷺ) - since in the Book of Allaah and the *Sunnah* of His Messenger (ﷺ) lies your success (if you cling to them if you attest to the truth of what they inform of and follow their commands) in this world and the Hereafter.

Servants of Allaah...
There are some people who doubt and seek to cause doubts that sins are a cause of misfortunes, and that is because of the weakness of their *eemaan* and their negligence in reflecting upon the Book of Allaah, the Mighty and Majestic, and I will recite for the benefit of such people the saying of Allaah, the Mighty and Majestic:

وَلَوْ أَنَّ أَهْلَ ٱلْقُرَىٰٓ ءَامَنُوا۟ وَٱتَّقَوْا۟ لَفَتَحْنَا عَلَيْهِم بَرَكَٰتٍ مِّنَ ٱلسَّمَآءِ وَٱلْأَرْضِ وَلَٰكِن كَذَّبُوا۟ فَأَخَذْنَٰهُم بِمَا كَانُوا۟ يَكْسِبُونَ ﴿٩٦﴾ أَفَأَمِنَ أَهْلُ ٱلْقُرَىٰٓ أَن يَأْتِيَهُم بَأْسُنَا بَيَٰتًا وَهُمْ نَآئِمُونَ ﴿٩٧﴾ أَوَأَمِنَ أَهْلُ ٱلْقُرَىٰٓ أَن يَأْتِيَهُم بَأْسُنَا ضُحًى وَهُمْ يَلْعَبُونَ ﴿٩٨﴾ أَفَأَمِنُوا۟ مَكْرَ ٱللَّهِ فَلَا يَأْمَنُ مَكْرَ ٱللَّهِ إِلَّا ٱلْقَوْمُ ٱلْخَٰسِرُونَ ﴿٩٩﴾

"And if the people of the towns had believed and had *taqwaa* (piety), certainly, We should have opened for them blessings from the heavens and the earth, but they belied (the Messengers). So we took them (with punishment) for what they used to earn (polytheism, and crimes etc.). Did the people of the towns then feel secure against the coming of Our punishment by night while they are asleep? Or, did the people of the towns then feel secure against the coming of Our punishment in the forenoon while they play? Did they then feel secure against the plot of Allaah. None feels secure from the plot of Allaah except the people who are lost."[22]

One of the Pious Predecessors (*Salaf*) said: "If you see Allaah grant blessings to a certain person, and then you see that person continuing in disobedience to Him, then know that this is from Allaah's plan against him and that he is referred to by Allaah, the Most Highs, saying:

"We shall gradually seize them with punishment in ways they perceive not. And I respite them; certainly My plot is strong."[23]"

O Muslims, O worshippers of Allaah:
By Allaah, sins affect the security of a land; they affect its ease; its prosperity; its economy; and they affect the hearts of its people. Sins cause alienation between the people. Sins cause one Muslim to regard his Muslim brother as if he were upon a separate religion other than Islaam.

But if we sought to rectify ourselves, our families, our neighbours and those in our areas, and everyone we are able to rectify, if we mutually encouraged good and forbade evil, if we assisted those who do this with wisdom and wise admonition - then it would produce unity and harmony. Allaah, the Mighty

---

22 Soorah al-A'raaf (7):96-99

23 Soorah al-A'raaf (7):182-183

and Majestic, says:

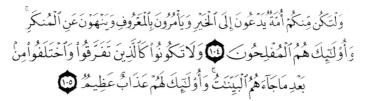

"Let there arise out of you a group of people inviting to all that is good (Islaam), enjoining the *ma'roof*[24] and forbidding the *munkar*[25]. And it is those who are successful. And be not as those who divided and differed among themselves after the clear proofs had come to them. It is they for whom there is an awful torment."[26]

I call myself and you, O my brothers, to come together upon the *Deen* of Allaah, the Mighty and Majestic; support one another in establishing the *Sharee'ah* of Allaah; advise each other sincerely with wisdom and wise admonition; debate with those whom we have to debate with in the best way and by satisfying them with textual proofs and intellectual proofs and do not abandon the people of false beliefs upon their falsehood since they have a right upon us that we should explain the truth to them and encourage them to follow it and that we explain what is false to them and warn them against it.

But as for remaining a disunited nation having no regard for one another and not caring about the affairs of each other then whoever does not care about the Muslims is not from them.

O Muslims, I say and repeat that it is binding upon us, being Muslims and Believers that we see the occurences and misfortunes from the Islamic

---

24 *Ma'roof: Tawheed* (making all worship for Allaah alone) and all that Islaam orders one to do.

25 *Munkar: Shirk* (associating others with Allaah in worship), *Kufr* (disbelief) and all that Islaam has forbidden.

26 Soorah Aali-'Imraan (3):104-105

perspective as shown by the Book of Allaah and the *Sunnah* of His Messenger (ﷺ). Since if we look at them from a materialistic perspective then the unbelievers are stronger and greater than us in the materialistic sense and they hold sway over us and enslave us through that. However, if we look from an Islamic perspective by way of the Book and the *Sunnah* then we will abandon all that is a cause of these misfortunes, and if we return to Allaah and aid the *Deen* of Allaah, the Mighty and Majestic, then Allaah says in His Book, and He is the most truthful in speech and most capable, He, the Mighty and Majestic, says:

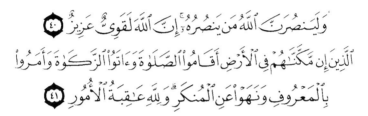

"Verily, Allaah will help those who help His (cause). Truly, Allaah is All-Strong, All-Mighty. Those (Muslim rulers) who, if We give them power in the land, (they) order the establishment of prayer and the payment of Zakaat,[27] and they enjoin the *ma'roof*[28] and forbid the *munkar*[29]. And with Allaah rests the end of (all) matters (of the creatures)."[30]

He did not say "those whom if We give them power in the earth establish arenas of sin, idle frivolity and shamelessness" rather he said:

$$\text{ٱلَّذِينَ إِن مَّكَّنَّٰهُمۡ فِي ٱلۡأَرۡضِ أَقَامُواْ ٱلصَّلَوٰةَ وَءَاتَوُاْ ٱلزَّكَوٰةَ وَأَمَرُواْ بِٱلۡمَعۡرُوفِ وَنَهَوۡاْ عَنِ ٱلۡمُنكَرِۗ وَلِلَّهِ عَٰقِبَةُ ٱلۡأُمُورِ ٤١}$$

---

27 The obligatory charity.

28 See footnote no. 24

29 See footnote no. 25

30 Soorah al-Hajj (22):40-41

"Those (Muslim rulers) who, if We give them power in the land, (they) order the establishment of prayer and the payment of Zakaat, and they enjoin the *ma'roof* and forbid the *munkar*. And with Allaah rests the end of (all) matters (of the creatures)."

Consider carefully, O Muslim brother, how Allaah, the Mighty and Majestic, said:

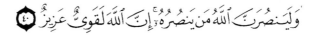

"Verily, Allaah will help those who help His (cause). Truly, Allaah is All-Strong, All-Mighty."

He stressed this promise of help with terms of emphasis: an implicit oath, the letter *laam* of emphasis, and the *noon* of emphasis. He further emphasised it by His saying:

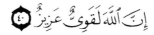

"Truly, Allaah is All-Strong, All-Mighty."

Since by His Power and His Might He helps those whom He wills, and consider how He ended the two *Aayahs* with His saying:

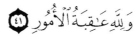

"And with Allaah rests the end of (all) matters (of the creatures)."

So a person may say due to his faulty thinking: "how can we be aided and granted victory against these unbelieving nations which are stronger and more powerful than us." So Allaah, the Most High, explains that the affairs are under His control only and that He has power over everything. We all know what effect earthquakes have - occurring when Allaah, the Mighty and Majestic, has ordered:

"Be! and it is."[31]

and such huge and all embracing destruction occurs in a single second as cannot be produced by the strongest of these nations.

By Allaah, if we truly aided Allaah's *Deen* as we aught to then we would be granted victory over every enemy upon the earth, but unfortunately many of us are appendages of the enemies of Allaah and the enemies of His Messenger (ﷺ) - observing their actions against Allaah and His Messenger (ﷺ) then following them in that. Perhaps even going to their lands and tossing our own flesh and blood - sons and daughters - into those lands where nothing is heard but church bells... wherein no *adhaan*[32] is heard... no mention of Allaah, the Mighty and Majestic, is heard... and nothing is seen except sin and idle frivolity...

So we ask Allaah, the Most High, that He turns the misguided of this *Ummah* back to the guidance, and that He makes us all to support one another and aid one another in carrying out good and righteousnous until we return to this *Ummah* its lost glory and honour. Indeed He is one fully able and having the power to do that.

O Allaah accept from us (our righteous deeds). Indeed You are the one who hears and knows everything.

O Allaah accept from us (our righteous deeds). Indeed You are the one who hears and knows everything.

O Allaah accept from us (our righteous deeds). Indeed You are the one who hears and knows everything.

---

[31] Soorah an-Nahl (16):40

[32] *Adhaan*: The call to prayer.

O Allaah, extol Muhammad and his true followers and family as You extolled Ibraaheem and the family of Ibraaheem. Indeed You are worthy of all praise, the most noble.

O Allaah, send blessings upon Muhammad and upon his true followers and family as You sent blessings upon Ibraaheem and the family of Ibraaheem. - indeed You are Worthy of all Praise, the Most Noble.